The Stuff Dreams Are Made Of.

Proudly supplying the equipment that helps the
dreams of future champions come true. Since 1884.

Louisville Slugger®

HδB. Hillerich & Bradsby Co., Louisville, Kentucky.

Say yes to sports, say no to drugs!

Louisville Slugger®

LOS ANGELES DODGERS

BILL SHANNON

BONANZA BOOKS

New York

First published in 1991 by Bonanza Books, distributed by Outlet Book
Company, Inc., a Random House Company, 225 Park Avenue South,
New York, New York 10003, by arrangement with MBKA.

Louisville Slugger is a registered trademark
of Hillerich & Bradsby Company, Louisville, Kentucky

This book has not been authorized by, and is not an official publication
of, the Los Angeles Dodgers. The views represented are those of the author.

ACKNOWLEDGMENTS

Majority of Player Photographs by Tom Dipace
Additional thanks to:
John Broggi—JKJ Sports Collectibles, Inc.
National Baseball Hall of Fame & Museum, Inc.

Printed and bound in the United States of America

Library of Congress Cataloging-in-Publication Data

Shannon, Bill.
    The Los Angeles Dodgers / by Bill Shannon.
        p.   cm. — (Louisville Slugger)
    Summary: An overview of the Los Angeles Dodgers baseball team,
discussing its history, last season, great moments, records, and
prospects.
        ISBN 0-517-05787-5
    1. Los Angeles Dodgers (Baseball team)—Juvenile literature.
[1. Los Angeles Dodgers (Baseball team)]   I. Title.   II. Series.
GV875.L6S47   1991
796.357′64′0979494—dc20   90-28324
                                                              CIP
                                                               AC

ISBN 0-517-05787-5

8   7   6   5   4   3   2   1

CONTENTS

TOM LASORDA

MANAGER

If there is anyone who has become a fixture with the Los Angeles Dodgers, it is Tommy Lasorda. Now in his 43rd season with the organization, Lasorda has been the manager for 15 years after serving as a player (mostly in the minors) for 11 seasons, a scout for four years, a minor league manager for eight years, and a coach in Los Angeles for four more (1973-76). Lasorda is now the senior manager in the majors in terms of consecutive seasons with the same team. During his years at the helm, the Dodgers have won six Western Division championships, turning four of them into National League pennants and converting two of those into world championships (1981 and 1988). Lasorda began his major league managing career with a bang, winning pennants in each of his first two seasons after succeeding longtime field boss Walter Alston. In 1977 and 1978 Lasorda guided the Dodgers to NL pennants and became only the second manager in the history of the league to win pennants in his first two seasons. (Gabby Street had performed the feat with the St. Louis Cardinals nearly a half-century before, and five American League managers had also done it.) Lasorda had also been a very successful minor league manager, finishing first five times and second twice in eight seasons. He won his 1,000th major league game as a manager on August 27, 1988, and later that season led the Dodgers to one of the most exciting World Series victories in history, upsetting the Oakland Athletics in five games. His 1981 Series triumph came at the expense of the New York Yankees. Last season the Dodgers finished strong for Lasorda but were unable to overcome the huge early lead built by the Reds. Now he will have a chance to rebuild the Dodgers' fortunes around slugger Darryl Strawberry and, perhaps, a recovered Orel Hershiser.

TIM BELCHER
PITCHER

The loss of Orel Hershiser last season would have been less crippling if Belcher had been healthy. The right-hander had been the Dodgers' second most effective pitcher for the two seasons prior to 1990. Belcher was originally drafted in the first round of the 1984 January draft by the New York Yankees, but he was lost a week after his signing when the Oakland A's claimed him as free-agent compensation. He came to Los Angeles in September 1987 for left-hander Rick Honeycutt. He made his major league debut shortly after the trade and was an immediate success, winning four of six decisions. In 1989 his eight shutouts were a major league high, and he finished only one strikeout behind National League leader Jose DeLeon. Belcher had proved to be particularly resourceful late in the season. He finished 1988 with nine wins in his final 11 decisions. He capped that by beating the Mets twice in the National League playoffs and going 1-0 in the World Series. In 1989 Belcher won his last seven decisions. He was 5-0 with a 1.51 ERA in September. That final spurt gave him a career-high 15 victories. Throughout 1990, however, he was plagued by arm woes. They limited him to 24 starts and 153 innings, his lowest major league totals since 1987. Though his ERA was 4.00, he did manage to strike out 102 batters, a total that suggests his arm strength is still present. The Dodgers need a Belcher comeback in 1991, particularly if Hershiser fails to rebound.

Age: 29			Bats: Right						Throws: Right	
	W	L	SV	G	CG	IP	HA	BB	SO	ERA
1990	9	9	0	24	5	153.0	136	48	102	4.00
Career	40	29	5	105	19	596.2	491	186	477	3.12

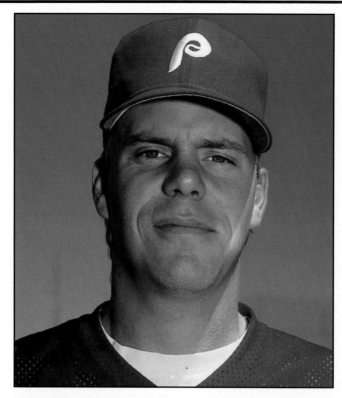

DENNIS COOK

PITCHER

A graduate of the University of Texas, Cook was chosen by the San Francisco Giants in the 18th round of the 1985 draft. With future major leaguers Greg Swindell and Bruce Ruffin in the university's starting rotation, Cook had been used as a reliever and outfielder. He was transformed into a starter after signing with the Giants. In 1987 he was named the Texas League (double-A) Pitcher of the Year after going 9-2 with a 2.13 ERA for Shreveport. He made his major league debut with a win against the San Diego Padres on September 9, 1988. He split two other well-pitched decisions. Cook opened the 1989 season with triple-A Phoenix and was 7-4 with 85 strikeouts in 78 innings when he was recalled by San Francisco. His stay with them was short. After winning his first decision, Cook found himself the key figure in a four-player deal that brought relief ace Steve Bedrosian from the Phillies to the Giants. He went 6-8 with Philadelphia, yet he threw well. In his best start he beat the Expos with a 3-0 hitter on September 29, 1989. Cook pitched inconsistently for the Phillies in 1990, and he was victimized by poor run support. With their pitching staff beset by injuries, the Dodgers traded top catching prospect Darrin Fletcher for Cook in midseason. His performance was good enough to give L.A. hope for 1991. Cook could be an important Dodger pitcher, especially if Hershiser and Belcher fail to regain their form.

Age: 28				Bats: Left				Throws: Left		
	W	L	SV	G	CG	IP	HA	BB	SO	ERA
1990	9	4	1	47	2	155.3	155	56	64	3.92
Career	18	13	1	74	5	299.0	274	105	144	3.76

TIM CREWS

PITCHER

No, he's not Tom Cruise, though throughout much of the 1990 season the Dodgers found this right-hander to be every bit as attractive as the matinee idol. Crews was the Dodgers' chief set-up man in 1990. Though his numbers were not overwhelming at first glance, he was among the team's most consistent pitchers. He posted career bests in games (66), innings pitched (107⅓), and strikeouts (76). His five saves were a career high, and his 2.77 ERA was second only to Jay Howell's. Crews was originally signed by Milwaukee in January 1981. He and Tim Leary came to the Dodgers on December 10, 1986, in the deal that sent Greg Brock to the Brewers. A career minor league starter at that point, Crews was sent to Albuquerque as a reliever, and he excelled in the role. He was recalled by the Dodgers in July 1987. He allowed only one run in his first 18 major league innings. Crews pitched briefly for Albuquerque again in 1988 but was recalled by L.A. on May 13. He was undefeated in four decisions. He was especially impressive in the closing days of that season's pennant race. He allowed only one earned run in his final seven games. In 1990, with the Dodger rotation in disarray, Crews made two starts. It was his first work as a starter since pitching for Vancouver, a Milwaukee farm club, in 1986. He will probably remain in the bullpen in 1991, especially if Mike Hartley is pressed into the starting rotation.

Age: 30				Bats: Right					Throws: Right	
	W	L	SV	G	CG	IP	HA	BB	SO	ERA
1990	4	5	5	66	0	107.1	98	24	76	2.77
Career	9	7	9	172	0	269.2	274	71	197	2.94

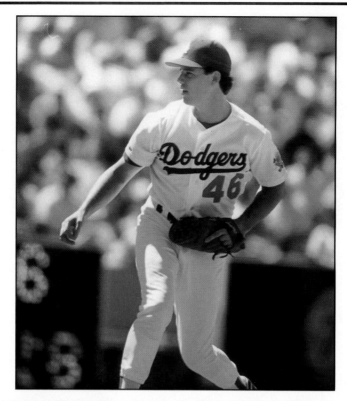

MIKE HARTLEY
PITCHER

Hartley was originally signed by the Cardinals on November 27, 1981. On December 9, 1986, Los Angeles drafted him from Savannah, a St. Louis farm team, for its minor league club in San Antonio. Hartley had been used primarily as a starter until 1986, when he was converted into a reliever. The Dodgers continued to utilize him in that role. Splitting his time between Bakersfield (California League) (Class A), San Antonio (Texas League) (double-A), and Albuquerque (triple-A), Hartley went 8-8 with 18 saves. In 99 innings he struck out 112 while walking only 48. He started 1988 with Albuquerque but was uncharacteristically wild and was sent down to San Antonio. The setback was brief. In 45 innings Hartley went 5-1 with nine saves, 57 strikeouts, 18 walks, and an 0.80 ERA. He was named the Texas League's pitcher of the month for June. Shortly afterwards he was recalled by Albuquerque. The reliever spent most of 1989 in triple-A. Glowing numbers (7-4, 18 saves, 2.79, 76 strikeouts in 77⅓ innings) won him a promotion to the Dodgers. He made his major league debut at San Diego on September 10, 1989. Hartley opened the 1990 season on the major league roster. Though used primarily as a set-up man for Jay Howell, he was pressed into the starting rotation when injuries crippled the Dodger pitching staff. He performed impressively in both roles. His six wins included his first major league shutout. He's another possible starter for the 1991 Dodgers.

Age: 29			Bats: Right						Throws: Right	
	W	L	SV	G	CG	IP	HA	BB	SO	ERA
1990	6	3	1	32	1	79.1	58	30	76	2.95
Career	6	4	1	37	1	85.1	60	30	80	2.85

OREL HERSHISER
PITCHER

Are the Dodgers now paying the price for Hershiser's past success? Hershiser was the National League's Cy Young Award winner in 1988, when he went 23-8 and pitched a major league record 59 consecutive scoreless innings. He also pitched a career-high 267 innings. He followed that with a grueling work load during post-season play. Hershiser pitched 8⅓ innings against the Mets on October 4. Four days later he pitched seven innings. The following night he pitched in relief. On October 12 he clinched the NL pennant with a shutout of New York. Four days later he pitched another complete-game shutout, against Oakland in the World Series. On October 20 he threw yet another complete game and clinched the Series for L.A. Then in 1989 he threw 256⅔ innings while finishing at 15-15. A lack of run support contributed heavily to his .500 record; Hershiser's 2.31 ERA was the second lowest in the National League. Last season he was beset by arm woes. The former workhorse started only four games and pitched 25⅓ innings. He was soon placed on the disabled list—an injury to his right rotator cuff ended his season. It was an irreparable blow to the Dodgers, though they recovered nicely enough to throw a late season scare into Cincinnati. However, they were finally undone by their pitching. A healthy Hershiser might have meant a division title for Los Angeles. Will he recover? Although he did some light tossing in September, the Dodgers won't know the answer until after spring training.

Age: 32			Bats: Right						Throws: Right	
	W	L	SV	G	CG	IP	HA	BB	SO	ERA
1990	1	1	0	4	0	25.1	26	4	16	4.26
Career	99	65	5	235	58	1482.1	1266	438	1027	2.71

JAY HOWELL
PITCHER

For the first four years of Jay Howell's major league career, managers couldn't decide whether he was a starter or a reliever. He saw infrequent action in either role with three major league clubs during that time. Howell came into his own in 1984, when Yankee manager Yogi Berra put him in the bullpen as Dave Righetti's primary set-up man. He struck out 109 batters in 103⅔ innings while winning nine games and posting a 2.69 ERA. He also saved seven games in limited opportunities. Those numbers caught the attention of the Oakland Athletics. The A's, desperate for a closer, insisted that Howell be included as part of the Yankee package that brought Rickey Henderson to New York. Howell saved 45 games in his first two seasons with Oakland (1985, '86). In 1987 he saved 16 more games, but his ERA soared to 5.89. Plagued by arm miseries, he lost his closer's role to Dennis Eckersley. He was dealt with shortstop Alfredo Griffin to Los Angeles shortly after the season ended. Howell's 21 saves helped the Dodgers to a world championship in 1988. He was even better in 1989, when his 28 saves set a Dodger single-season record and his 1.58 ERA was a career low. Howell was almost untouchable in Dodger Stadium that summer. He had 16 saves and a 1.16 ERA at home. Injuries limited him to 45 appearances in 1990, but he was effective when he took the mound. Howell led the team in saves (16) and he struck out 59 batters in 66 innings.

Age: 35			Bats: Right						Throws: Right	
	W	L	SV	G	CG	IP	HA	BB	SO	ERA
1990	5	5	16	45	0	66.0	59	20	59	2.18
Career	44	41	133	389	2	645.0	610	230	531	3.43

RAMON MARTINEZ
PITCHER

For the last four years, Martinez was one of the most highly touted prospects in the Dodger organization. In 1990 he delivered on the promise. Martinez was signed as a free agent when he was only 16 years old. Though he was blessed with vast reserves of raw talent, his skills needed honing. He gradually worked his way up the minor league ladder and made his major league debut with the Dodgers in 1988. Though he showed a live fastball in his six starts, he struggled with his control. He started the following year with triple-A Albuquerque. He was already a 10-game winner when he was called up by the Dodgers in mid-season 1989. Martinez became a member of the starting rotation after Tim Leary was traded to Cincinnati for Kal Daniels. He went 6-4. His victories included two complete-game shutouts against the Atlanta Braves. On September 15 he had what was at that time a career-high 12 strikeouts against Atlanta. The Braves were his victims again on June 4, 1990, when Martinez tied Sandy Koufax's Dodger record for most strikeouts in a nine-inning game (18). He got even better as the season progressed. He led the league with 12 complete games and was tied for second in the NL strikeout race. He also finished third in innings pitched, and that is some cause for concern. Heavy workloads have proved to be detrimental to many young arms. The Dodgers should be more cautious.

Age: 23		Bats: Right						Throws: Right	
	W	L	SV	G	CG	IP	HA	BB	SO	ERA
1990	20	6	0	33	12	234.1	191	67	223	2.92
Career	27	13	0	57	14	368.2	297	130	335	3.08

MIKE MORGAN

PITCHER

Though he has pitched well for the last two years, Mike Morgan is still searching for his first winning season as a major leaguer. He was signed by the Oakland A's in 1978 and was traded to the Yankees two years later. After a 7-11 season with New York in 1982, he was dealt (along with Fred McGriff and Dave Collins) to the Toronto Blue Jays. He spent most of his Blue Jay tenure (1983-84) with their Syracuse farm club. That was followed with stints with the Seattle (1985-87) and Baltimore (1988) organizations. His major league record stood at 34-68 with a whopping 4.90 ERA when he was traded by the Orioles to L.A. for Mike Devereaux on March 11, 1989. Morgan started the 1989 season in the Dodger bullpen, but he quickly won a place in the rotation. He got off to a hot start. By the end of May he was 4-2 with a league-leading 1.19 ERA. But then he lost nine of his next 11 starts. A lack of runs was the chief culprit in Morgan's defeats. For instance, his ERA for June 1989 was 2.43, but he won only once in six decisions. However, he did pitch poorly after the All-Star break and was relegated to the bullpen for the remainder of the season. A sparkling 2.53 ERA did not prevent an 8-11 record. Runs were still at a premium for Morgan in 1990, and he again finished below .500. He did, however, tie for the team lead in starts. His 211 innings pitched also placed him second on the club behind Ramon Martinez.

Age: 31			Bats: Right						Throws: Right	
	W	L	SV	G	CG	IP	HA	BB	SO	ERA
1990	11	15	0	33	6	211.0	216	60	106	3.75
Career	53	94	2	230	30	1149.0	1251	406	520	4.37

PAT PERRY

PITCHER

Perry was first signed by the Houston Astros in January 1978. That contract was the beginning of a baseball odyssey that has seen the left-hander pitch for 12 teams in five different organizations. He made his major league debut with the St. Louis Cardinals on September 12, 1985, when he allowed only two hits in four innings of a crucial game against the New York Mets. Four days later he nailed his first big league win against the Pittsburgh Pirates. Perry split the 1986 season between St. Louis and Louisville (triple-A). He started 1987 with the Cards and went 4-2 as a long reliever but was traded to Cincinnati on August 31. The Reds sent him to the Chicago Cubs on May 19, 1988. He hit his first major league home run in his first Cub at-bat on August 6. Perry was an ideal left-handed specialist for Chicago. He enjoyed a great start in 1989. After allowing three earned runs in his first appearance on April 5, he then pitched 21⅓ consecutive scoreless innings. He allowed earned runs in only three of his initial 19 appearances. Perry also stranded 17 of 22 inherited runners. Sadly, his season came to a halt when a sore left shoulder placed him on the disabled list on June 17. Perry was not reinstated to the active roster until September 29. He had surgery to repair his left rotator cuff on November 9. The Dodgers signed him as a free agent on January 26, 1990. Still recovering, Perry was used sparingly last season.

Age: 32				Bats: Left					Throws: Left	
	W	L	SV	G	CG	IP	HA	BB	SO	ERA
1990	0	0	0	7	0	6.2	9	5	2	8.10
Career	12	10	6	182	0	263.0	215	99	131	3.46

KEVIN GROSS

PITCHER

With all the question marks on their pitching staff, the Dodgers felt a dire need to get someone who could give them 200 or more innings. So they signed Gross as a free agent on December 3, 1990. The right-hander was brought up to the majors by the Philadelphia Phillies in 1983. He was traded to the Expos for Floyd Youmans and Jeff Parrett just prior to the 1989 season and spent the next two summers in Montreal. He has not been a big winner. His 15 victories in 1985 were a career high, and they came in his last winning season. His record has been over .500 in only one other year. He is, however, a workhorse. As a Phillie and an Expo, Gross strung together five consecutive 200-inning seasons (1985–89). That streak ended last year when the Expos used him briefly in the bullpen and passed over him in several starts after he pitched poorly. Gross was a member of the 1988 National League All-Star Team. He may have received his greatest notoriety during the 1987 season: He was suspended for 10 days when umpires discovered he had been using a tack to scuff up the baseball. Upon signing him, Dodger general manager Fred Claire said, "We feel Kevin adds a great deal of talent and experience to our starting pitching. . . .he has the ability to be a major contributor." Throughout their history, the Dodgers have had excellent luck in reviving the careers of discarded pitchers. Perhaps their magic will work again with Gross.

Age: 29				Bats: Right				Throws: Right		
	W	L	SV	G	CG	IP	HA	BB	SO	ERA
1990	9	12	0	31	2	163.1	171	65	111	4.57
Career	80	90	1	265	29	1469.1	1447	583	996	4.02

JOHN WETTELAND
PITCHER

Wetteland was once as highly touted as Ramon Martinez, but his career took a step backward in 1990. He was originally signed by Los Angeles as the second selection in the 1985 draft. Wetteland had his best minor league season in 1987, when he won 12 games for Vero Beach (Class A) and finished fourth in the league in strikeouts (144). Following that year, he was drafted by Detroit, but he was returned to Los Angeles when he failed to make the Tigers' major league roster. Assigned to San Antonio (double-A), Wetteland was named Texas League Player of the Month in May 1988 and was a starting pitcher in that league's All-Star game. He reached triple-A Albuquerque in 1989. In 10 starts with that club, he was 5-3 with 73 strikeouts in 69 innings. Wetteland made his major league debut on May 31 in relief against the Montreal Expos. He started his first major league game against Atlanta on June 5. He pitched five innings, allowing two runs on two hits, but failed to get a decision. He beat Houston for his first major league win on June 15. Wetteland was inserted into the Dodger starting rotation in late July. He finished the season 5-8, but had 96 strikeouts with only 34 walks in 102⅔ innings. He was expected to be a regular starter in 1990, but he could not crack L.A.'s rotation. When he did pitch for the Dodgers, he performed erratically. Wetteland has been the subject of trade rumors. This season may be his last chance with L.A.

Age: 24			Bats: Right						Throws: Right	
	W	L	SV	G	CG	IP	HA	BB	SO	ERA
1990	2	4	0	22	0	43.0	44	17	36	4.81
Career	7	12	1	53	0	145.2	125	51	132	4.08

FERNANDO VALENZUELA
PITCHER

Despite throwing the first no-hitter of his career, Valenzuela suffered his fourth consecutive mediocre season. His 4.59 ERA was his worst ever and he surrendered more hits than innings pitched for only the second time in his career. On the plus side, his control—which had been horrendous for the past three seasons—showed dramatic improvement. His five complete games and two shutouts represented his best totals since 1987. Such modest accomplishments underscored the tremendous decline in Valenzuela's game. Fernando captured the national imagination when he opened 1981 with eight consecutive wins, a total that included seven complete games. His 13-7 mark during that strike-torn summer helped him become the first pitcher to win the Rookie of the Year and Cy Young Awards in the same season. He went on to be named to six All-Star games. In 1986, Valenzuela won a career-high 21 games and finished second to Mike Scott in the Cy Young Award voting. That same season, he tied Carl Hubbell's All-Star Game record by striking out five consecutive batters. The following year, at the age of 26 years and five months, he became the second youngest Dodger to win 100 games. Don Drysdale was four months younger when he accomplished the feat. A return to Valenzuela's former luster is a must for 1991. With the Dodger pitching staff top heavy with starters he will have to fight for a spot in the rotation.

Age: 30				Bats: Left					Throws: Left	
	V	L	SV	G	CG	IP	HA	BB	SO	ERA
1990	13	13	0	33	5	204	223	77	115	4.59
Career	141	116	2	331	107	2348	2094	915	1759	3.31

MIKE SCIOSCIA
CATCHER

Scioscia was the Dodgers' first-round pick in the 1976 draft. He joined Los Angeles in 1980 as an understudy to Steve Yeager and in 1982 became the Dodgers' primary catcher. Scioscia enjoyed one of his finest years at the plate in 1990. He set career highs in home runs (12) and RBIs (66) while batting .264. It was his second straight year of home runs in double figures. Prior to 1989 he had never hit more than seven homers in any single season. Although Scioscia's home runs have been infrequent, Dodger fans won't soon forget one of them. On October 9, 1988, Scioscia hit a game-tying shot against New York Met ace Dwight Gooden in the fourth game of the National League playoffs. The dramatic blow came in the ninth. The Dodgers won the game in extra innings to knot the series, which they eventually won. Scioscia hit .364 in those playoffs. The post-season heroics were something of a surprise. He had hit only .257 with three home runs during the regular season. He has hit as high as .296 (1985), but his bat has never played a large role in his reputation. His greatest value is realized behind the plate. Scioscia is a mobile catcher. Though he is not gifted with the league's strongest arm, he compensates with a quick, accurate release. Dodger pitchers treasure his game-calling ability. At 6'2", 223 pounds, enemy base runners find him an immovable object at home, and he is renowned as the most fearless plate blocker in the majors.

Age: 32			Bats: Left					Throws: Right				
	G	AB	H	2B	3B	HR	R	RBI	BB	SO	SB	AVG.
1990	135	435	115	25	0	12	46	66	55	31	4	.264
Career	1205	3680	963	176	7	57	340	382	488	244	22	.262

ALFREDO GRIFFIN
SHORTSTOP

Griffin joined the Dodgers on December 11, 1987. He was part of the blockbuster three-way deal that turned Bob Welch and Matt Young into Oakland A's; sent Jack Savage, Wally Whitehurst, and Kevin Tapani to the New York Mets; and brought Jay Howell and Jesse Orosco to the Dodgers. Griffin was one of the better shortstops in baseball at the time of the trade. He had come up to the majors as a Toronto Blue Jay and in 1979 had been a co-recipient of the AL Rookie of the Year Award (with Minnesota third baseman John Castino). He was also a former All-Star and Gold Glove winner. In three seasons with Oakland, he batted .273 with 83 stolen bases. His tenure with Los Angeles has been somewhat disappointing. He did provide the club with much-needed defense in their 1988 world champion-ship season, but he spent 57 days on the disabled list. (An errant Dwight Gooden fastball crushed the second metacarpal on his right hand on May 21.) He didn't return to the lineup until late July, and his hitting suffered all season. Griffin batted better in 1989 (.247), but he stole only 10 bases. He did, however, hit a career-high 27 doubles. In the field his .975 fielding average was also a career best, but he seemed to sacrifice range. His decline was more apparent in 1990, when his .210 batting average was the third lowest of his career. With Jose Offerman ready to fulfill his destiny at shortstop, Griffin will be hard-pressed for playing time in 1991.

Age: 33			Bats: Both					Throws: Right			
	G	AB	H	2B	3B	HR	R	RBI	BB	SO	SB	AVG.
1990	141	461	97	11	3	1	38	35	29	65	6	.210
Career	1744	6185	1548	229	76	24	696	487	304	584	184	.250

LENNY HARRIS

THIRD BASE

Harris was originally signed by the Cincinnati Reds as a fifth-round choice in the 1983 June draft. From 1983 to 1987 he played throughout Cincinnati's minor league system. Though a fine defensive infielder, particularly at third base, Harris failed to impress with the bat. However, he did win notices on the base paths. He stole 119 bases in his first five minor league seasons. In 1988 he was sent on loan to Glen Falls (Detroit Tigers). He batted .338 in 17 games and was promptly called up by Cincinnati's Nashville (triple-A) farm club. He went on to enjoy his finest professional season to that point. Batting .277, Harris led the American Association with 45 stolen bases. He was promoted to the Reds on September 2, and on September 19 got his first major league hit, off San Diego's Ed Whitson. He had six multi-hit games in 12 Cincinnati starts. Harris started 1989 with the Reds as a utility infielder. Hitting just .223, he was traded with Kal Daniels to the Dodgers for pitcher Tim Leary and infielder Mariano Duncan on July 18. His bat picked up with L.A., and he was an especially effective pinch hitter (8 for 20 and a .500 on-base percentage). In 1990 Harris had his best season ever. Used primarily at third, he was second on the Dodgers in hitting, fourth in runs scored, and tied for third in stolen bases. He might be even more productive in 1991. Harris enters the season as the odds-on favorite to win the starting third basemen's job.

Age: 26			Bats: Left							Throws: Right		
	G	AB	H	2B	3B	HR	R	RBI	BB	SO	SB	AVG.
1990	137	431	131	16	4	2	61	29	29	31	15	.304
Career	268	809	226	27	5	5	104	63	54	68	33	.279

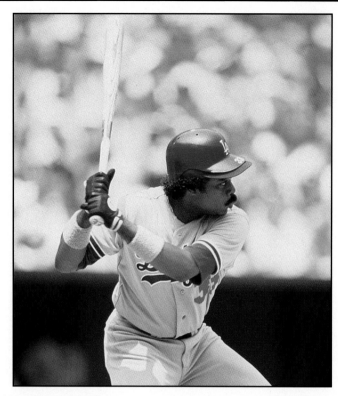

EDDIE MURRAY
FIRST BASE

Murray staged an astounding comeback in 1990. The former perennial All-Star had been in a three-year decline prior to the start of the year. His once Gold Glove reflexes had slowed in the field, and his batting skills had obviously eroded. An Oriole from 1977 to 1988, Murray joined the Dodgers for the 1989 season. He managed to lead the team in RBIs (88) that summer, but he batted only .247. It was the worst season of his career. However, he erased the ugly memories of it in 1990, finishing second in the NL batting race by hitting a career-high .330 and driving in a team-leading 95 RBIs. (Had he won the race, Murray would have been the Dodgers' first batting titlist since Tommy Davis in 1963.) Besides batting and RBIs, Murray led his team in home runs (26), runs (96), and walks (82). His .414 on-base percentage was third in the league behind Lenny Dykstra (.418) and Dave Magadan (.417). Murray's 184 hits were the second highest total of his career. The first baseman has been a prolific slugger since 1977, when he won the AL Rookie of the Year Award. He has hit 20 or more home runs in 13 different seasons. Among switch hitters, Murray's 379 home runs place him second to Mickey Mantle on the all-time list. His RBI-per-game percentage is among the best in modern baseball history. He has driven in 84 or more runs in every season he has played except for strike-torn 1981, when he led the American League with 78.

Age: 35			Bats: Both						Throws: Right		
	G	AB	H	2B	3B	HR	R	RBI	BB	SO	SB	AVG.
1990	155	558	184	22	3	26	96	95	82	64	8	.330
Career	2135	7997	2352	402	29	379	1210	1373	1026	1076	76	.294

JUAN SAMUEL

SECOND BASE

Samuel's career is in jeopardy. From 1984 to 1987, as a second baseman with the Philadelphia Phillies, Samuel was considered one of baseball's more electrifying offensive forces. He posted double figures in doubles, triples, and home runs in each of those seasons while stealing at least 35 and as many as 72 bases. Few players could boast of his combination of speed and power. Though his lack of walks made him a less than ideal leadoff man, Samuel scored more than 100 runs three times and had 100 RBIs in 1987. His hitting faltered in 1988, when Philadelphia experimented with him at third base and in the outfield. Still slumping, he was traded to the New York Mets for Roger McDowell and Lenny Dykstra on June 18, 1989. The Mets made him their starting center fielder, a position Samuel never relished. His fielding—never a strong point—and hitting suffered. He finished the year with full-season career lows in almost every offensive category. It was thought that the post-season trade to the Dodgers would revivify his career. Stuck in center field once again, Samuel got off to a horrendous start. After the trade of Willie Randolph to the Oakland A's, Samuel returned to second base and his hitting did improve somewhat. However, his fielding was below major league caliber. He managed to lead the team with 38 stolen bases, but he was caught stealing 20 times, the third highest total in the league.

Age: 30			Bats: Right						Throws: Right			
	G	AB	H	2B	3B	HR	R	RBI	BB	SO	SB	AVG.
1990	143	492	119	24	3	13	62	52	51	126	38	.242
Career	1081	4328	1116	213	75	116	622	493	283	1026	318	.258

MIKE SHARPERSON
INFIELD

With the Dodgers juggling their infield during 1990 to find the right defensive combination, Mike Sharperson finally got the chance to properly showcase his talents. The infielder posted career highs in games played and at-bats and in every offensive category. His .376 on-base percentage was the fourth highest on the Dodgers. That shouldn't have come as too much of a surprise, since he had exhibited a good batting eye while in the minor leagues. Sharperson started his professional career by signing with the Toronto organization in June 1981. (He had previously been drafted by three other teams.) He joined the Blue Jays as their starting second baseman in 1987 but hit only .208 in 32 games. In a rare display of impatience, Toronto sent him down to the minors. Though he batted .299 for triple-A Syracuse (International League), he was traded to Los Angeles for pitching prospect Juan Guzman on September 21. He finished the 1987 season with L.A. and batted .273 in 10 games. He spent most of 1988 and 1989 at triple-A Albuquerque. He hit over .300 both seasons but found his path to employment in Los Angeles blocked by Steve Sax, Alfredo Griffin, and Willie Randolph. Like Lenny Harris, Sharperson could be a victim of the Strawberry factor in 1991. If Jose Oferman lives up to his advance billing, Sharperson will have a hard time gathering at-bats unless he can triumph over both Harris and Samuel in the infield sweepstakes.

Age: 29		Bats: Right						Throws: Right			
	G	AB	H	2B	3B	HR	R	RBI	BB	SO	SB	AVG.
1990	129	357	106	14	2	3	42	36	46	39	15	.297
Career	244	573	158	24	3	3	63	55	62	78	17	.276

BRETT BUTLER
CENTER FIELD

For a sustained outburst of hitting, Brett Butler was a prize winner in 1990. Over his last 30 games Butler hit .368, and over his last 44 games, .374. This surge enabled him to raise his batting average from .295 on September 1 to .309 (the second highest of his career) by the end of the season. (His career-best was .311 for the 1985 Cleveland Indians.) He missed his career-high in stolen bases by just one, stealing 51 (in 70 attempts). (He had 52 for the Indians in 1984). It was the third straight season he had led the Giants in stolen bases. Over those final 30 games, he stole 14 bases in 18 attempts. Interestingly, Butler led all Giant hitters in walks by a wide margin, with 90 (next was Will Clark, with 62). He was also the Giants' most durable player, playing in 160 games (Matt Williams played in 159). Butler even improved in the area of grounding-into-double-plays. In 1989 he hit into four DPs, an outstanding figure. He actually improved on that last season by grounding into only three. He also gave the Giants some defensive solidarity in the midst of chaos when the team was rife with injuries. It is also no coincidence that the Giants have had the league leader in RBIs in each of the last three seasons. Those are the three seasons Butler has been with the team. In those three years he has scored 317 runs in 471 games, an average of .673 runs per game getting on base ahead of Clark, Kevin Mitchell, and Williams. Butler, by signing as a free agent with the Dodgers, has added a dimension to the Los Angeles attack, giving the club the pure leadoff man it has been seeking since the defection of Steve Sax via the free agent route.

Age: 30			Bats: Left						Throws: Left		
	G	AB	H	2B	3B	HR	R	RBI	BB	SO	SB	BA
1990	160	622	192	20	9	3	108	44	90	62	51	.309
Career	1360	5001	1424	189	83	39	850	363	654	527	358	.285

KAL DANIELS
OUTFIELD

Daniels was originally selected by the New York Mets in the third round of the 1982 January draft. The club failed to sign him. Cincinnati then successfully drafted him in the secondary phase of the 1982 June draft. In his first year of pro ball with Billings of the Pioneer League (Class A), Daniels hit .367 and led the circuit in stolen bases (27) and game-winning RBIs (nine). He was named to the All-Star team and began a rapid ascent through the Reds' minor league system. After hitting .371 with triple-A Nashville in less than half a season, Daniels was called up by Cincinnati on June 29, 1986. He batted .320 in 181 big league at-bats. A hamstring injury in September kept him from further mistreating NL pitchers. A month on the disabled list in 1987 also limited his numbers, but he still managed to hit .334 with 26 home runs and 26 stolen bases in only 368 at-bats. In 1988 he led the NL with a .397 on-base percentage. But 1989 was a painful season for him. His sore knees handicapped him at the plate and in the field, and he was traded to L.A. in the Tim Leary deal. He hit well for the Dodgers until the pain became intolerable. He submitted to surgery on August 7 and was lost for the season. He made a fine comeback in 1990. He led the Dodgers in home runs (27) and slugging (.531) and reestablished himself as one of the top hitters in baseball. His still-weakened knees did handicap him in the field, however, and he was held to a career-low four stolen bases in seven attempts.

Age: 27		Bats: Left							Throws: Right		
	G	AB	H	2B	3B	HR	R	RBI	BB	SO	SB	AVG.
1990	130	450	133	23	1	27	81	94	68	104	4	.296
Career	507	1665	500	99	7	81	316	262	280	323	81	.300

JOSE GONZALEZ

OUTFIELD

Gonzalez was signed by the Dodgers as a 16-year-old in 1980 and was sent to Lethbridge in the Rookie League in 1981. He batted only .136 that season but hit .301 for the same team in 1982. He also drove in 47 runs in only 55 games. A promotion to Class A Lodi came the following season. Gonzalez batted .294, but a thumb injury ended his summer. Returning to Class A in 1984, his still-healing thumb held him to .221, though he stole 49 bases and was second on the team with 11 home runs. He was promoted to San Antonio in 1985. A Texas League All-Star, Gonzalez batted .306 with 13 home runs, 62 RBIs, and 34 stolen bases. The performance earned him a late-season Dodger call-up. He batted .273 with two doubles in 11 at-bats. His fielding was, as it has been throughout much of his career, exemplary. Back in triple-A Albuquerque in 1986, he hit .277 with 37 RBIs in 89 games. The Dodgers recalled him in mid-season but used him sparingly. This established a pattern. Gonzalez was shuffled between triple-A and Los Angeles for the next three years. In 1988 he hit .306 for Albuquerque and stole 44 bases in only 84 games. In 1989 he batted .268 in 261 at-bats for the Dodgers, yet he failed to win a regular job. Last season was particularly frustrating. Gonzalez appeared in a career-high 106 games but batted only 99 times. With Darryl Strawberry joining L.A. and with Stan Javier's emergence, 1991 does not bode well for the former prospect.

Age: 26			Bats: Right								Throws: Right	
	G	AB	H	2B	3B	HR	R	RBI	BB	SO	SB	AVG.
1990	106	99	23	5	3	2	15	8	6	27	3	.232
Career	337	504	121	26	6	7	76	33	40	124	25	.240

CHRIS GWYNN
OUTFIELD

Gwynn was a collegiate superstar. In 1984 he set the NCAA Division 1 record for hits in a season (137). He still holds the San Diego State single-season records for runs (95), total bases (243), RBIs (95), and triples (nine). He was a member of the All-Western Conference and NCAA All-America first teams. He was also named to the U.S. Olympic baseball team for the games played in Dodger Stadium in 1984. He was signed by Los Angeles in the 1985 June draft. Gwynn has steadily moved up the Dodger chain, though his progress has been retarded by his lack of power. He hit well in the minor leagues, but he had little to show for it in the way of run production. He rarely coaxed a base on balls, and he was not a base-stealer. In three brief tours with L.A. (1987, '88, and '89), Gwynn had few chances to impress the Dodger management. He was named the top rookie in L.A.'s 1989 spring-training camp, but he still started the season in the minors. He was recalled on April 30. Injuries to his right foot and knee held him to only 32 games. Gwynn did make some strides last year. His .284 batting average and 141 at-bats were major league highs for him, and he showed surprising power with five home runs. As a left-handed hitter who can play all three outfield positions, Gwynn will probably be the Dodgers' primary pinch hitter and outfield reserve in 1991. He is the brother of perennial National League batting champion Tony Gwynn.

Age: 26			Bats: Left							Throws: Left	
	G	AB	H	2B	3B	HR	R	RBI	BB	SO	SB	AVG.
1990	101	141	40	2	1	5	19	22	7	28	0	.284
Career	162	252	65	7	2	5	30	31	11	46	1	.258

STAN JAVIER
OUTFIELD

Originally a New York Yankee, Javier was part of the exchange that sent Rickey Henderson to the Big Apple in December 1984. Javier saw little playing time in his first two years with the A's and was used chiefly as a pinch runner and defensive specialist. In 1988 he became a semi-regular, gathering 397 at-bats in 125 games. He batted .257 and stole 20 bases in 21 attempts. He was impressive in 1988 post-season play. He hit .500 in both the AL playoffs and the World Series. He came to spring training with the 1989 A's as the favorite to win the left fielder's job. A poor start at the plate and the return of Rickey Henderson ended his hopes. In 1990 Javier was stuck on the Oakland bench when the Willie Randolph trade sent him to Los Angeles. At the time of the deal, Kirk Gibson was still recovering from leg injuries, and the Dodgers were using Kal Daniels and Hubie Brooks to patrol left and right fields. Both were cursed with limited range. Los Angeles was desperate for a center fielder who could cover a lot of ground. Javier was given the job, and he responded both in the field and at the plate. He hit a career-high .304. His .384 on-base percentage was the third highest mark on the club. Though he batted only 276 times, he scored 56 runs. His defense was superb. The good glove runs in the family: Javier's father, Julian, was the brilliant second baseman for the great St. Louis Cardinal clubs of the 1960s.

Age: 25			Bats: Both						Throws: Right		
	G	AB	H	2B	3B	HR	R	RBI	BB	SO	SB	AVG.
1990	123	309	92	9	6	3	60	27	40	50	15	.298
Career	507	1288	323	45	13	8	187	107	138	219	58	.251

DARRYL STRAWBERRY
OUTFIELD

There is little doubt that Darryl Strawberry will add a special dimension to the Dodgers' offense in 1991. One of the game's truly consistent power hitters, Strawberry was perhaps the most significant free-agent signee of the off-season, and the Dodgers got him. During his eight-year career with the New York Mets, Strawberry averaged 31.5 home runs and 91.6 RBIs per season. Although the subject of seemingly constant criticism in New York for what were perceived as his lapses in the field, Strawberry brings to Los Angeles the most unusual commodity in baseball—a lethal bat. The 1990 season was one of his best, although he was sidelined in the closing stages with a back injury that was not considered severe. He set a Mets' single-season club record for RBIs (108) and became the only player in the history of the team to drive in 100 or more runs three times, having also done it in 1987 and 1988. He was chosen for the NL All-Star team for the seventh straight season, and when he departed the Mets, he was the club's all-time career leader in home runs, RBIs, extra-base hits, and runs scored. Even though Strawberry missed the final week of the season, he still had a notable September, hitting five of his 37 homers in the season's final month. Two of those homers helped keep alive the Mets' slender hopes of winning their division. On September 11 he beat the Cardinals with a two-run ninth-inning shot, and two days later he delivered a three-run homer off Doug Drabek that wiped out a Pirates' lead and led the Mets to a 6-3 victory. He had a slow start last season, batting only .230 on May 25 but ran through a couple of typical hot streaks. He had four homers in three games in early June and 11 RBIs in eight games later in the month.

Age: 29						Bats: Left					Throws: Left	
	G	AB	H	2B	3B	HR	R	RBI	BB	SO	SB	AVG.
1990	152	542	150	18	1	37	92	108	70	110	15	.277
Career	1109	3903	1025	187	30	252	662	733	580	960	191	.263

1990 SEASON

Under ordinary circumstances, finishing 10 games over .500 and five games behind the Cincinnati Reds might not be considered a successful season by Los Angeles Dodgers' standards. But 1990 was anything but an ordinary year for the Dodgers. In some ways, it was perhaps the best managerial job of Tommy Lasorda's 14 seasons.

Things started badly, and got worse. By July 23 the Dodgers were third—but a distant third, 13 games behind the Reds—and given virtually no hope of moving into a position to seriously contend for the West title.

Orel Hershiser had been expected to be a major factor in the pitching plans despite his 15-15 record in 1989, but an injury took him out of those plans, and Tim Belcher, another pitcher expected to make a heavy contribution, was also sidelined for part of the season. Hershiser appeared in only four games and was 1-1.

Of the pitchers who were healthy all year, rookie Ramon Martinez was easily the biggest contributor to the second-half surge. Martinez finished 20-6, one of only three 20-game winners in the National League, and tied with New York's Dwight Gooden for second in the strikeout derby with 223 (the Mets' David Cone had 233). He also led the league in complete games with 12. It was fortunate that he had as many route-going games as he did, since the Dodger bullpen was inconsistent. Jay Howell led the club with only 16 saves (despite a 2.18 ERA), and he had just six of them after August 15. Tim Crew had five saves, the next best on the club.

What made the season a positive one was the way the Dodgers finished. Despite all their pitching problems, they had a very strong second half and actually put pressure on the front-running Reds down the stretch, something that most observers thought impossible midway through the season. From the low point on July 23, the Dodgers were on fire, chopping 10 games off the Reds' 13-game bulge by September 14.

Losing Belcher for the final six weeks of the campaign may have been the death knell for the Dodgers' beleaguered pitching staff, but it was really the inconsistency of the bullpen that made the whole season an uphill climb.

Los Angeles held leads of at least three runs in games it ultimately lost a staggering 11 times. Two of those were memorable. On August 21, the Dodgers had an 11-1 lead over the Phillies—and lost, 12-11. Against Houston two weeks later, the Dodgers led, 7-0; the Astros eventually won the game, 10-8.

Still, there were several positive signs in the pitching area in addition to Martinez. The emergence of rookie right-hander Mike Hartley was certainly one of them. Hartley won his first major league start on August 14 at New York (besting Cone by the score of 2-1) and finished at 6-3. Jim Neidlinger, another right-handed rookie, had a five-game winning streak and was 5-2 overall.

Mike Morgan pitched well in spots but wound up 11-15 with a 3.75 ERA, although he did give the Dodgers 211 innings, which helped relieve some of the pressure on the bullpen.

Part of the pitching problems, of course, stemmed from an unsettled infield, where veterans Juan Samuel and Alfredo Griffin were disappointments. Both were displaced by rookies in the closing stages of the season.

On the hitting side, there were some positives. Stan Javier performed well in center field and batted .304, although he had only 276 at-bats. Javier was used as a leadoff man much of the second half and may find a job in that role. He doesn't have much power (3 homers, 24 RBIs), but he does have some speed.

Utilityman Mike Sharperson also had a good season at the plate, batting .297, but also had little punch (3 homers, 36 RBIs in 357 at-bats).

Eddie Murray was the biggest offensive news. The switch-hitting first baseman put on a great drive to help lift the Dodgers after the All-Star break. Over that span, Murray batted almost .360 and hit 15 of his 26 homers. He made a determined bid in the season's closing days to win the batting title, winding up second with .330 (missing Willie McGee's frozen figure of .335). He also had 95 RBIs, 53 of them coming after the break. Murray had to be nine for nine in the last two games of the season to catch McGee. As it was, he went five for eight, which just got him close.

On the less positive side was the saga of Kirk Gibson. Gibson, the NL MVP in his first season with the Dodgers (1988) and the author of the remarkable ninth-inning pinch-hit home run that helped the Dodgers to their dramatic World Series victory, was a one-man disaster area. He was not only hounded by injuries again (in 1989 he appeared in only 71 games), but he also lost favor with the fans for what seemed to be his lackadaisical play in the field. Gibson finished at .260 with eight home runs and 38 RBIs.

But the Gibson problem was even worse than that. He became a disruptive force on the club. At midseason, he had a highly publicized argument with general manager Fred Claire and demanded to be traded. After that simmered down, he had a run-in with one of the announcers on the television crew in August, which generated more negative publicity. Then he was benched by Lasorda.

Gibson also resented the boos from the Dodger Stadium crowds who felt that his effort, particularly in the field, was not up to the standards of his $1.5 million salary.

Finally, Gibson declared that he would become a free agent, with the intention of returning to a club closer to his native Michigan. It was clear that the disappointed Dodgers weren't prepared to do much to prevent his departure.

On the other hand, ex-Red Kal Daniels appeared quite happy in L.A. and turned in a solid all-around performance that included 27 homers and a near-.300 season. He also became the first Dodger hitter to collect three grand-slam home runs in a season since 1977 (when Roy Cey did it).

Lenny Harris was another Dodger who prospered during the season, batting .302 and helping to ease the uncertainty at second base created by the departure of Willie Randolph to Oakland.

Overall, the offensive performance was adequate, and the defense gave some signs of settling down as the season progressed. But historically the Dodgers have lived and died by their pitching. In 1990 they died by it. Had Belcher's shoulder stayed healthy, had Howell not experienced knee problems, and had Hershiser been a part of the rotation, things could have been very different at Dodger Stadium. As it was, the Dodgers did not have enough arms left to maintain a rotation.

One of the most difficult parts of the season for many Dodger watchers was the performance of Fernando Valenzuela. Once the star of the staff and the dominant left-hander in the league, Valenzuela struggled all year. He finally finished with a break-even record (13-13) and struck out 115 in 204 innings, but he had a 4.59 ERA, the highest of his 11-year career with the Dodgers. His previous worst came during an injury-ridden 1988, when his ERA was 4.24. Although he is now only 30, Valenzuela's Dodger days appear over. After having won 141 games for the club since 1980, he will probably become a free agent, and the Dodgers don't seem prepared to sign him.

When all was done, Lasorda had every reason to be proud of a team that was seemingly out of the race by July 4 yet still managed to finish with a rush and put some pressure on Cincinnati, the division leader throughout the entire season.

Ramon Martinez

HISTORY

The history of the Dodgers begins in another league, in another century, and on another coast. Back in the 1880s a man named Charlie Byrne sought to take advantage of the great enthusiasm in the city of Brooklyn over the relatively new sport of baseball.

Brooklyn, located across the East River from New York, was not yet a part of that metropolis. Indeed, it was a thriving and independent city. It was also a city filled with baseball teams—the Excelsiors, the Atlantics, and the Putnams, to name just a few.

For one season a professional club was located in Brooklyn—the Mutuals, who played at Union Grounds—but they were owned by a man named William Cammeyer, who thought it better to identify them as "New York" rather than "Brooklyn." A couple of other teams had been members of the loosely organized pro circuit called the National Association, and the "New York" Mutuals had been in the National League in 1876.

But none of these teams lasted. Byrne established a club that joined the American Association (at the time the rival major league to the NL), and the club not only survived, it blossomed. After winning the AA championship in 1889 and facing the New York Giants in the World Series, the Brooklyn club jumped into the NL in 1890—and promptly won the pennant again. Thus, Brooklyn had the unique distinction of winning the pennant two straight years in two different leagues.

After Byrne died, the team went through several ownership shuffles. Harry von der Horst, Ned Hanlon, and Charles Ebbets became the major owners. The first two were also involved with the original Baltimore Orioles, the strongest team in the NL in the 1890s, and they shifted a lot of their stars to Brooklyn, where pennants were won in 1899 and 1900 with Hanlon as the manager.

Brooklyn was absorbed into the rest of New York City in 1898, but the ballclub continued to be known as Brooklyn.

With Ebbets now in control, the team built a new ballpark,Ebbets Field, which opened in 1913. Another of the old Orioles, Wilbert Robinson, became the manager in 1914 and began to rebuild the team. In 1916 and 1920 the Dodgers (as they were to become known) won the NL flag but lost the World Series, to the Red Sox and the Indians respectively.

Initially, most teams did not have nicknames, being known simply by the name of the city they represented, "the New Yorks," "the Brooklyns," etc. But when the Dodgers played in old Washington Park, the field was surrounded by streetcar, or trolley, lines. The club became known as the "Trolley Dodgers," because players and fans had to "dodge" their way around whizzing streetcars to get into the park.

For a while, the Dodgers were known by other names: the "Bridegrooms," because a lot of the players were newlyweds; the "Robins," in honor of Wilbert Robinson; but it always came back to Dodgers, and finally the name stuck.

After the 1920 championship season, the team declined into the lower reaches of the NL and became something of a laughingstock. Changing managers (Max Carey, Casey Stengel, etc.), did little good.

But then a new general manager, Larry MacPhail, arrived on the scene, and things began to change. In 1938 MacPhail installed lights in Ebbets Field. It just so happened that Cincinnati's Johnny Vander Meer pitched a no-hitter against the Dodgers in the first night game there (June 15). It was Vander Meer's second consecutive no-hitter.

MacPhail put the Dodgers on the radio for the first time, with Red Barber as the lead announcer. He brought in Gladys Goodding as the first regular ballpark organist. He also hired firey Leo Durocher as the manager. In 1941 the Dodgers won the pennant for the first time in 21 years.

After MacPhail became part owner of the Yankees and left Brooklyn, Branch Rickey took over running the club and, in 1947, made history by signing Jackie Robinson as the first black player in modern baseball history.

With Robinson, Duke Snider, Roy Campanella, Don Newcombe, Carl Furillo, Gil Hodges, Carl Erskine, and a host of other stars, the Dodgers became a post–World War II powerhouse. Pennants were won in 1947, '49, '52, '53, '55, and '56. In 1955 the Dodgers won the World Series for the first time, beating the Yankees four games to three.

In 1957 owner Walter O'Malley decided the club could no longer stay in the now cramped and decaying Ebbets Field and so moved the team to Los Angeles, where a new era of Dodger history began.

Led by such pitching greats as Sandy Koufax and Don Drysdale and great hitters like Tommy Davis, the Dodgers once again became a dominant team in the 1960s. Managed by Walter Alston, the Dodgers won pennants in 1959, '63, '65, '66, and '74.

After Alston retired in 1976 (following 23 years as manager), Tommy Lasorda took over as the field boss. He quickly guided the Dodgers to two more flags—1977 and 1978. But it wasn't until 1981 that the Dodgers again won the Series. With a team that starred Pedro Guerrero, Steve Garvey, Ron Cey, Davey Lopes, and Bill Russell, the Dodgers defeated the Yankees in 1981. In 1988 a Lasorda-managed team again won the Series, this time defeating the Oakland Athletics behind the pitching of Orel Hershiser.

One of the most dramatic moments in World Series history came in the ninth inning of the first

Jackie Robinson

game of that series, when an injured Kirk Gibson, barely able to walk, hobbled to the plate as a pinch hitter and slugged a game-winning homer off relief ace Dennis Eckersley. Other heroics later came from reserve Mickey Hatcher, among others, but it was the brilliant pitching of Hershiser that stood out.

After moving to Los Angeles, the Dodgers played for four seasons in the L.A. Coliseum, where the football configuration of the stadium led to a short left field with a high screen. Then in 1962 the team opened lovely Dodger Stadium in Chavez Ravine. It remains one of the premier ballparks in the major leagues, set in a scenic area and engineered for outstanding comfort and viewing.

Today the Dodgers, now run by Walter O'Malley's son, Peter, are one of the best-known and most popular of all major league teams and have received great support from the fans of the Los Angeles area. The Dodgers were the first team to draw over 3 million and have drawn more fans over the last 20 years than any other club.

The Natural: A nearly crippled Kirk Gibson pinch-hits a game-winning ninth inning home run off Oakland's Dennis Eckersely with two men out. It was recently voted the Greatest Moment in LA Dodger History (October 15, 1988)

1990 TEAM LEADERS

BATTING

Eddie Murray

Games	Eddie Murray	155
At-bats	Hubie Brooks	568
Batting average	Eddie Murray	.330
Runs	Eddie Murray	96
Hits	Eddie Murray	184
Doubles	Hubie Brooks	28
Triples	Lenny Harris, Stan Javier	4
Home runs	Kal Daniels	27
On-base percentage	Eddie Murray	.414
Slugging percentage	Eddie Murray	.520
RBIs	Eddie Murray	95
Total bases	Eddie Murray	290
Walks	Eddie Murray	82
Most strikeouts	Juan Samuel	126
Stolen bases	Juan Samuel	38
Caught stealing	Juan Samuel	20

1990 TEAM LEADERS

PITCHING

Games .... Tim Crews   66

Wins.......................... Ramon Martinez   20

Losses .... Mike Morgan   15

Starts .... Ramon Martinez,
                                      Mike Morgan,
                        Fernando Valenzuela   33

Complete games .... Ramon Martinez   12

Shutouts .... Mike Morgan   4

Innings .... Ramon Martinez   234 ⅓

ERA .... Ramon Martinez   2.92

Strikeouts .... Ramon Martinez   223

Walks .... Fernando Valenzuela   77

Saves .... Jay Howell   16

Relief appearances .... Tim Crews   66

Winning percentage .... Ramon Martinez   .769

Hits allowed .... Fernando Valenzuela   223

1990 TRANSACTIONS

DATE	PLAYER	TRANSACTION
March 30	Dave Hansen	Optioned to Albuquerque
	Jose Offerman	Optioned to Albuquerque
	Braulio Castillo	Optioned to San Antonio
	Isidrio Marquez	Optioned to San Antonio
	Dan Opperman	Optioned to San Antonio
	Zak Shinall	Optioned to San Antonio
March 31	Kirk Gibson	Placed on 15-day disabled list (left hamstring)
	Pat Perry	Placed on 21-day disabled list (left shoulder)
April 1	Terry Wells	Acquired from Houston for Franklin Stubbs
April 7	Jim Gott	Placed on 15-day disabled list (right elbow)
	Jeff Bittiger	Outrighted to Albuquerque
	Mike Maddux	Outrighted to Albuquerque
	Don Aase	Purchased from Albuquerque
	Mike Munoz	Purchased from Albuquerque
April 8	Darrin Fletcher	Optioned to Albuquerque
	Terry Wells	Optioned to Albuquerque
April 16	Rick Dempsey	Placed on 15-day disabled list (sprained back)
	Kirk Gibson	Moved to 21-day disabled list (left hamstring)
	Carlos Hernandez	Purchased from Albuquerque
April 21	Jeff Hamilton	Placed on 15-day disabled list (small partial tear to right rotator cuff)
	Jim Gott	Moved from 15 to 21-day disabled list
	Brian Traxler	Purchased from Albuquerque
April 23	Jay Howell	Placed on 21-day disabled list (left knee)
	Pat Perry	Moved from 21-day to 30-day disabled list
April 24	Jose Vizcaino	Purchased from Albuquerque
April 27	Orel Hershiser	Placed on 60-day disabled list (right shoulder)
April 30	Jose Vizcaino	Optioned to Albuquerque
May 3	Rick Dempsey	Reinstated from 15-day disabled list
	Carlos Hernandez	Optioned to Albuquerque
May 4	Jim Gott	Begins 30-day Rehabilitation assignment
May 11	Mike Munoz	Optioned to Albuquerque
	Mike Maddux	Purchased from Albuquerque
May 13	Pat Perry	Begins 30-day rehabilitation assignment
	Stan Javier	Acquired from Oakland for Willie Randolph
May 14	Ray Searage	Placed on 15-day disabled list (retroactive to May 11; left elbow)
	Mike Munoz	Recalled from Albuquerque
May 17	Jay Howell	Reactivated from 21-day disabled list
	Mike Munoz	Optioned to Albuquerque
May 22	Pat Perry	Reinstated from 30-day disabled list
	Brian Traxler	Optioned to Albuquerque
	Jeff Hamilton	Moved from 15-day to 21-day disabled list
May 25	Jim Gott	Reinstated from 21-day disabled list
	Mike Hartley	Optioned to Albuquerque
June 2	Kirk Gibson	Reinstated from 21-day disabled list
	John Shelby	Given unconditional release
June 8	Ray Searage	Begins 30-day rehabilitation assignment
June 11	Pat Perry	Placed on 15-day disabled list (left shoulder tendinitis)
	Ray Searage	Moved from 15-day to 21-day disabled list
	Mike Hartley	Recalled from Albuquerque
June 13	Mike Maddux	Outrighted to Albuquerque
	Jim Poole	Purchased from San Antonio

DATE	PLAYER	TRANSACTION
June 21	John Wetteland	Optioned to Albuquerque
	Jose Vizcaino	Recalled from Albuquerque
	Jeff Hamilton	Moved from 21-day to 60-day disabled list
	Pat Perry	Moved from 15-day to 21-day disabled list
July 2	Terry Wells	Recalled from Albuquerque
	Jim Poole	Optioned to San Antonio
	Ray Searage	Reinstated from 21-day disabled list
	Don Aase	Placed on 21-day disabled list (right rotator cuff tendinitis)
July 31	Terry Wells	Optioned to Albuquerque
	Jim Neidlinger	Purchased from San Antonio
August 11	Dave Walsh	Purchased from Albuquerque
	Jose Vizcaino	Optioned to Albuquerque
August 17	Tim Belcher	Placed on 15-day disabled list (right shoulder tendinitis)
August 18	Jose Offerman	Recalled from Albuquerque
	Ray Searage	Placed on 15-day disabled list (retoractive to August 15; inflammation of medial collateral ligament in left elbow)
	Don Aase	Reinstated from 21-day disabled list
September 1	Darrin Fletcher	Recalled from Albuquerque
	Darren Holmes	Purchased from Albuquerque
	Jim Poole	Recalled from San Antonio
	Jose Vizcaino	Recalled from Albuquerque
	Pat Perry	Reinstated from 21-day disabled list
September 10	Tim Belcher	Placed on 60-day disabled list (right shoulder)
September 11	Ray Searage	Reinstated from 15-day disabled list
September 12	Dave Hansen	Recalled from Albuquerque
	Carlos Hernandez	Recalled from Albuquerque
	Luis Lopez	Purchased from Albuquerque
	John Wetteland	Recalled from Albuquerque
September 13	Dennis Cook	Acquired from the Philadelphia Phillies in exchange for catcher Darrin Fletcher
September 21	Barry Lyons	Signed as a free agent

Kirk Gibson

1991 ASSESSMENT

Darryl Strawberry. Because of that name, the whole ballgame has changed for the Los Angeles Dodgers. This team has been built historically around speed and pitching. Now, however, the Dodgers have not only Strawberry but also Eddie Murray, and this may add up to a lot of home runs. If they can back this up with their usual recipe of fine pitching, the Dodgers could be easy winners in the National League West.

Perhaps equally important as Strawberry to the Dodgers' potential success in 1991 is the recovery of Orel Hershiser, who missed virtually all of last season. A return to form by Hershiser, whose 23-8 season in 1988 was the primary reason for the Dodgers' winning the West, could help L.A. clinch it this time, too. With Hershiser anchoring the pitching staff and the heavy guns producing runs, the Dodgers could be as good as anyone in the division, and perhaps in the league.

Last season the Dodgers had a hot August and a fairly cold September and still finished only five games behind Cincinnati.

Los Angeles also struggled a bit on the road, finally finishing with a 39-42 mark, in contrast with Cincinnati's 45-36 mark away from Riverfront Stadium. At home the Dodgers were 47-34, a game better than the Reds, although their home record was only fifth best in the league.

Ramon Martinez had a great season, winning 20 of his 26 decisions and finishing tied for second in the league in strikeouts.

Slugging will cover some pitching deficiencies and defensive lapses, but over the course of a 162-game season it won't cover them all. Pitching was what carried the Dodgers a year ago.

A slight improvement in the pitching plus the addition of Strawberry will make the Dodgers a very formidable club. Even if Strawberry has his occasional defensive lapses, as his New York detractors say he does, his 30-plus homer output and 100-RBI level will more than compensate.

The Dodgers have some candidates for the role of protecting Strawberry and have to hope that they definitely find someone. Murray will probably hit third, ahead of Strawberry. Or Tommy Lasorda might opt to have Darryl hit third and, in that case, have Murray hit behind him. Either way, the No. 5 man in the order becomes one of the keys to the Dodgers' success.

There is another difficulty, and that is at shortstop, where Alfredo Griffin committed 26 errors last season. This means that switch-hitting rookie Jose Offerman, who made some appearances last season, is a likely candidate for the starting job. If the Dodgers are in the race late in the year and Offerman is the shortstop, his ability to keep his cool and field consistently will be one of the keys to their winning it.

But, overall, there is little question that the Dodgers have strengthened themselves considerably with the addition of Strawberry. The probable return of Hershiser will make them one of the favorites in the division.

PROSPECTS

HENRY RODRIQUEZ
Outfield

A left-handed hitting outfielder from Santo Domingo, Henry Rodriquez was perhaps the biggest single surprise in the entire Dodgers' farm system in 1990. On a team loaded with promising talent, Rodriquez became the star of double-A San Antonio when he blasted 28 homers and drove in 109 runs. He batted .291 and was named the MVP of the Texas League.

Rodriquez's development as a slugger was what caught everyone by surprise — he had hit only two home runs in his first two seasons in the minors. It may well be, however, that Rodriquez, who turned 23 in November, is a "late bloomer". That is, a player who realizes his strength and potential later in his career than some others.

After hitting no home runs in his first minor-league season in 1987 and two the next season, he improved in 1989, hitting 10 with Vero Beach, but still wasn't tabbed as a long-ball prospect by anybody.

Perhaps just as important, Rodriquez showed some selectivity at the plate last season when he drew 61 walks but struck out only 66 times for San Antonio. That's a very good ratio for a hitter who leads his league in home runs.

Rodriquez is a solid 180-pounder who, though primarily an outfielder, has played other positions as well during his minor league tour.

JOSE OFFERMAN
Shortstop

With regular Alfredo Griffin tied for the league lead among shortstops in errors with 26 in mid-September, 1990, Jose Offerman got a shot at the Dodgers' shortstop job in only his second season of professional ball.

Although Offerman homered in his first major league game, power is not something to be expected of him based on his minor league record. But it is one of the few things he apparently cannot do. Offerman was the MVP of the Pacific Coast League, in 1990, hitting .326 with Albuquerque and stealing 60 bases.

Offerman didn't hit a single homer at Albuquerque, but did have a .410 slugging percentage, with 11 triples among his 148 hits, and he had an on-base percentage of .416.

In 1989, Offerman split his season between single-A Bakersfield and double-A San Antonio. At Bakersfield, he was the All-Star shortstop, hitting .306 in 62 games through June with 15 extra-base hits and 37 steals. Shifted to San Antonio, he hit .288 in 68 games. His combined average for 130 games was .296 and he finished with 69 stolen bases.

Offerman also led the Dominican Winter League in stolen bases before reporting to Albuquerque last spring.

However, he may not be quite ready for the major league job defensively, having committed 36 errors in his 177 games in triple-A in1990. Nonetheless, he was one of the reasons why the Dukes won the PCL title with a 91-51 record.

This spring, he will be given every chance to win the starting role for the Dodgers who definitely see him as their shortstop for years to come. On opening day, Offerman will be only 22.

JIM POOLE
Relief Pitcher

Of all Henry Rodriquez's teammates at San Antonio, Jim Poole may be the most highly regarded in Los Angeles. The reason for this is simple: Poole is a left-handed reliever, a commodity the Dodgers have been desperately seeking since the halcyon days of Steve Howe.

Poole is a 6'2" former Georgia Tech pitcher who was selected by the Dodgers in the eighth round in June 1988. He began as a starter at Vero Beach but was converted in his second season there to the bullpen. He responded by posting an 11-4 record with 19 saves.

Last season at San Antonio, Poole continued his progress with 16 saves in 54 appearances, and although he had a 6-7 record, he was the only double-A player called up by the Dodgers in September. Poole had 77 strikeouts and only 27 walks in his 63 ⅔ innings at San Antonio and may fit a need for the parent club in 1991.

With L.A. last season, Poole appeared 16 times working 10 ⅔ innings without a decision or a save. In those appearances, he walked eight (but four of them were intentional) and struck out six. In four of the games in which he pitched, Poole finished up although he worked many in "mop-up" situations.

Poole will turn 25 in April and the Dodgers need to know if he has sufficient maturity to work in clutch major league situations. If he can, he may see a lot of service with the club in 1991.

OTHER DODGER PROSPECTS TO WATCH

Jim Neidlinger rattled around in the Pirates' system for five seasons, but may finally be getting a shot at a major league job. Obtained by the Dodgers in a swap with Pittsburgh after the 1988 season, Neidlinger was 8-6 in 1989 as a combination starter and reliever at Albuquerque.

In 1990 he became almost exclusively a starter (he made only two relief appearances) and he was 8-5 with an ERA of 4.29. However, light air and high scores at Albuquerque tend to distort earned-run marks and the Dodgers are impressed with the 26-year-old's size (he's 6'4").

Eric Karros accomplished a very difficult feat last season. On a team that featured plenty of talent including Henry Rodriquez, it was difficult for anyone to get much attention in San Antonio. Karros succeeded by winning the Texas League's batting title and being named the league's best defensive first baseman. Karros hit .352 with 18 homers and 78 RBIs. A 205-pounder from UCLA, Karros has been a consistent hitter throughout his three-year pro career. He batted .366 in 66 games at Great Falls in 1988 and .303 in 142 games at Bakersfield the following year.

One of the four sons of Manny Mota (now a Dodgers' coach), Domingo Mota could be a fast-track candidate for the Dodgers. He helped carry Cal State–Fullerton to the 1990 College World Series as a second baseman but was converted to the outfield by L.A. In the single-A Gulf Coast League, Mota hit .343, second best in the league.

Dan Opperman is a right-handed pitcher for whom the Dodgers have high hopes. Opperman was the club's first choice in the June, 1987, draft but missed his first two pro seasons with a pair of elbow operations. In 1989, he was 0-7 at Vero Beach. Last season, he was 12-8 with a 3.41 ERA in 27 starts at San Antonio.

Jose Offerman

Jim Neidlinger

KEY TRANSACTIONS

One of the more significant transactions in the early history of the Dodgers came about in a most peculiar way. In the late 1890s the National League was in something of a turmoil. It had 12 teams, and several of them were in small cities. These teams were not doing well at the gate, and a number of them wound up in the hands of owners who also owned other teams in stronger markets.

There was a tendency for these owners to shift players to the stronger team when the pennant race took shape, to enhance the chances of their better team to win. Perhaps the worst practitioners of this were the Robison brothers, who virtually stripped the Cleveland team of its quality players in order to strengthen the St. Louis Cardinals.

It turned out that the Dodgers were one of the beneficiaries of this "syndicate" style of baseball. Since their owners also owned the Baltimore Orioles, the Dodgers had a chance to improve themselves by the addition of some of the Baltimore stars.

When Oriole manager Ned Hanlon (one of the group involved in the ownership of the two teams) decided that Brooklyn was a better place to be based, he not only became the Dodgers' manager but also brought along such outstanding players as Wee Willie Keeler, Hugh Jennings, and Joe Kelley. Buttressed with this talent, the Dodgers, who had finished 10th and gone through three managers the year before, surged to the top of the NL in 1899. This transformation created a turnabout of 54 games in the standings: in 1898 the Brooklyn club finished 46 games out of first; in 1899 it won the pennant by eight games.

In 1900 the National League decided to reduce from 12 teams to eight, and Baltimore was among the four teams eliminated (as was Cleveland).

Because of their owners' decision, Brooklyn survived as a member of the NL and, indeed, won the pennant again in the first season of the eight-team circuit.

This transaction was easily the most important in the history of the club, because it involved the very survival of the Brooklyn Dodgers.

But the next most significant transaction in Dodger history, while it had great influence on the course of the team in the standings, assumed even greater significance in sociological terms.

During World War II Branch Rickey (the architect of the great St. Louis Cardinal teams) became the general manager of the Dodgers. Rickey was determined to sign one or more outstanding black players and break the unwritten but very pervasive color barrier that had been in effect in baseball for more than six decades. While the occasional black player had appeared in the minor leagues, the black playing talent was confined for all practical purposes to so-called Negro Leagues.

Rickey felt that many of the black players could help rebuild the Dodgers, but he also felt that the continued segregation of baseball was morally wrong. He was the son of a Methodist minister who, even while a big league catcher, had refused to play on Sundays, and he had seen segregation first-hand while playing college baseball with blacks who were not allowed to share accommodations with their white teammates.

Therefore, he set out to find some black players who could play in the major leagues. But he felt that those picked had to have special qualifications beyond playing skills. Rickey knew that they would be subjected to racial slurs before, during, and after games. He knew that attempts would be made to provoke them into angry or violent reactions. Rickey wanted to find black players who were skillful but also competitive and aggressive. However, he also wanted them to be mature and disciplined enough to take the abuse that he knew was sure to come without lashing out or becoming depressed and discouraged.

In short, these players needed not only major league athletic skills but also intense desire, moral fiber, and intelligence. His scouts and friends of the black community brought him one prospect after another, but all were rejected for being too young or too emotional.

Finally, he found Jack Roosevelt Robinson, a former college football player and a mature man who was still a fine athlete. Regrettably, many of the greatest of the black players in the Negro Leagues were past their prime and would not set the example of skill Rickey needed to make his experiment a success. Even Robinson was perhaps a little beyond the best age to begin a baseball career, but Rickey signed him in 1946 (when Jackie was already 27).

But Robinson proved to be the perfect choice. He was everything that Rickey hoped, and perhaps even more. After a season at Montreal in the Dodgers' farm system, Robinson joined the big league club for 1947—and was chosen as the major leagues' rookie of the year. He batted .297 and led the league in stolen bases (29), and the Dodgers won the pennant for the first time since 1941.

Rickey, of course, took a good deal of heat from his fellow owners, some of whom believed in segregation, and from some fans and even some members of the press for his bold move. But Robinson proved the point so conclusively that the Dodgers quickly added other fine black players to their roster, including pitchers Don Newcombe and Joe Black and catcher Roy Campanella.

Frank Robinson

During the balance of the 1940s and virtually all of the 1950s, the Dodgers' farm system produced a steady stream of talent, reducing the team's dependence on trades and waiver deals.

However, in an earlier era, after the death of several senior owners in the 1930s, Larry MacPhail, the flamboyant general manager of the Cincinnati Reds, was brought in to run the Dodgers. MacPhail moved to revive the team through a series of trades and waiver claims in which he produced several players who later became big Brooklyn favorites.

Included in this group were first baseman Dolph Camilli (acquired from the Phillies), outfielder Dixie Walker (from Detroit), and a veteran shortstop named Leo Durocher, who had been a member of the great New York Yankee teams of the late 1920s and had since played for several other clubs in both the majors and the minors.

MacPhail made Durocher the playing manager of the Dodgers in 1939, and the team moved from seventh to third that season, advancing to second place in 1940. By 1941 Durocher was phasing himself out of the shortstop position and moving in young Harold (Pee Wee) Reese, acquired in 1940 from Louisville in the Boston Red Sox organization. That season the Dodgers won their first pennant in 21 years.

During their years in Los Angeles, the Dodgers have made many trades of some interest, but the one that attracted the most attention was the acquisition of Hall of Fame slugger Frank Robinson from the Baltimore Orioles after the 1971 season. As it turned out, Robinson (the only man ever to be MVP in both leagues) was with the Dodgers for only one season (1972). However, when he was traded after that season to the California Angels, the Dodgers acquired a pitcher who was to help Walter Alston to his final pennant as Dodger manager—Andy Messersmith.

In 1974 Messersmith tied for the league lead in wins with 20 and hurled the Dodgers into the World Series against the Oakland Athletics. Unfortunately, Messersmith was the losing pitcher in two Series games that year. But he had helped give the Dodgers their first NL pennant in eight years.

During the era of free agency, the Dodgers made some acquisitions that proved to be very meaningful, though perhaps the one that garnered the most headlines was the signing of Kirk Gibson on January 29, 1988. Gibson not only won the NL MVP that year (the first for the Dodgers since Steve Garvey in 1974), but he also hit one of the most dramatic homers in World Series history. Gibson was injured late in the season, and his only World Series at-bat came in the ninth inning of the first game against the Oakland Athletics. The result was a game-winning homer off relief ace Dennis Eckersley.

GREAT MOMENTS

Perhaps the most memorable single moment in Dodger history came when owner Walter O'Malley announced after the 1957 season that the team was leaving Brooklyn, where it had been based since 1884, and was moving to Los Angeles.

This move had enormous implications for all of baseball, especially since the San Francisco Giants were another result of the move, as were, eventually, the New York Mets.

National League club owners had made it clear during the several years of negotiation between the Dodgers and New York City that they would not approve the move of a single ballclub from the East Coast to the West Coast. They felt that this would create enormous travel expense and scheduling problems that they could not endure. They suggested, however, that if *two* teams moved, then both moves might gain approval.

In August the New York Giants' board of directors, by a 9-1 vote, approved the move to San Francisco. But under the circumstances, no move was likely unless the Dodgers also moved. When O'Malley announced his decision, baseball suddenly became a truly national sport on the major league level.

Also, the void in New York was to ultimately lead to the creation of the New York Mets as an expansion team in 1962. Thus, at least three teams in the NL are where they are because of the Dodgers' decision, which was initially based on the inadequacy of Ebbets Field in Brooklyn.

However, the Dodgers have also provided their share of great moments on the field during their 100-year history.

Another memorable date in Dodger history came on October 4, 1955, at Yankee Stadium, when the Dodgers finally won the World Series for the first time. Although Brooklyn had won pennants in 1916, '20, '41, '47, '49, '52, '53, and '55, no Dodger team had ever been successful in a Series until that day.

Brooklyn's ultimate hero was Johnny Podres, the young left-hander who pitched the complete-game victory that afternoon. But he was aided enormously by a sparkling defensive play by Sandy Amoros, who turned Yogi Berra's bid for a double into a double play with a great running catch.

Thus came the end of a half-century of frustration. After all the previous World Series, Dodger fans had gone away saying, "Wait till next year!" Now, newspapers were filled with stories saying, "Next year has come!"

While the first season in Los Angeles was a nightmare for the Dodgers on the field (the team finished seventh, 21 games out of first), the 1959 season was a glorious one and produced more great moments. First was a playoff victory over the Milwaukee Braves, which got the club into the World Series. Then came the victory over the Chicago White Sox in six games, sealed when Larry Sherry earned the win in a 9-3 rout of the White Sox at Comiskey Park.

The Dodgers were to taste Series victory again in 1963 and 1965, giving L.A. three world championships in seven seasons.

In 1963 the victory was perhaps the sweetest of all, as the Dodgers smashed their long-time nemesis, the Yankees, in four straight games, with Sandy Koufax getting the victories in the first and fourth games. This was also the first World Series contested at Dodger Stadium, which had opened in 1962. The Dodgers scored only 12 runs in the four games, but their pitching staff held the mighty Yankees of Mickey Mantle, Roger Maris, Yogi Berra, Bill Skowron, and Elston Howard to just four runs—oddly, three of them allowed by Koufax.

After winning pennants in 1966, '74, '77, and '78 without a Series triumph, the Dodgers were to return to the pinnacle of the world's championship in 1981 under Tommy Lasorda.

In a season disrupted by a players' strike, the Dodgers played their way through a round of divisional playoffs as well as the NL championship series before reaching the World Series. They again confronted the Yankees, who had survived the two-tier playoffs in the American League.

It began as a disaster for the Dodgers, with New York winning the first two games at Yankee Stadium behind Ron Guidry and ex-Dodger Tommy John. By winning the third game behind young Fernando Valenzuela, 5-4, the Dodgers retained a glimmer of hope. Then the Series was even, as the Dodgers took the next game, 8-7, with Steve Howe getting the win in relief.

The Series took on a completely different shape when the Dodgers won the third game, 2-1, as Jerry Reuss outpitched Guidry. Then it was back to New York for the sixth (and final) game. With Burt Hooton's knuckle-curve baffling the Yankees, this one was a rout, 9-2.

One of the interesting twists of the 1981 Series was that the Dodgers swept the last four games and in the process defeated reliever George Frazier three times.

In 1988 the Dodgers were back in the Series. What was notable was the performance of two men—Kirk Gibson and Orel Hershiser. Gibson provided one of the most dramatic moments in Series history when he slammed a two-out, two-run pinch-hit home run in the ninth inning of the first game to give the Dodgers a 5-4 victory. Then it was Hershiser's turn. In Game 2, he shut out the powerful Oakland batting order for a 6-0 victory to put the Dodgers up two games to none. After the A's won the third game, Tim Belcher bested Dave Stewart in Game 4 to give the Dodgers a three-to-one edge.

Hershiser came back with a 5-2 victory in Game 5 in Oakland to end the Series and give the Dodgers their sixth world championship and fifth since the move to Los Angeles.

There have, of course, been many highlights in Dodger history that have not been related to the World Series, beginning with the team's entry into the National League in 1890 and the winning of the NL pennant that first year.

Then there was the opening of Ebbets Field, the team's first real permanent home, in 1913, and the first pennant in 1916, which led to the first World Series appearance.

In 1924 the Dodgers didn't win the pennant, but they set a club record by winning 15 games in a row. Babe Herman set a Dodger club record with a .393 average in 1930, but he didn't win the batting title (the Giants' Bill Terry hit .401).

One of the great highlights in the history of baseball, let alone that of the Dodgers, was the debut of Jackie Robinson in 1947. And Duke Snider provided plenty of heroics in the 1950s by hitting 40 or more home runs five straight seasons, including a club-record 43 in 1956.

After the move to Los Angeles, Sandy Koufax struck out 18 Giants in a game in 1959, a feat he was to repeat in 1962 against the Chicago Cubs. Koufax also pitched four no-hitters in the 1960s, including a perfect game on September 9, 1965, also against Chicago. He won the game, 1-0.

In 1968 Koufax's right-handed mate, Don Drysdale, set a record of 58 consecutive scoreless innings. Davey Lopes stole a record 38 straight bases in 1975, and Ron Cey had one of the most explosive months in baseball history when he drove in 28 runs in April 1977.

Manny Mota set a major league record for career pinch-hits in 1979. A year later Jerry Reuss pitched a no-hitter, and the Dodgers forced a playoff for the NL West title with a three-game sweep of the Houston Astros on the final weekend of the season.

In 1988 Orel Hershiser pitched 59 straight scoreless innings, breaking the record set nearly 20 years earlier by Drysdale.

And Dodger Stadium had a highlight of its own, without the Dodgers, when it hosted the baseball tournament for the 1984 Olympic Games.

This Is Next Year: Johnny Podres shuts out the Yankees
2-0 as the Dodgers finally win the World Series
(October 4, 1955)

ALL TIME ALL STAR TEAM

FIRST BASE ★ GIL HODGES

Except for parts of two seasons with the New York Mets, Gil Hodges played all of his 18-year career with the Dodgers. He was considered the finest first baseman of his time and was also one of the premier power hitters in the National League, slamming 370 career home runs and driving in 1,274 runs. Although originally a catcher, Hodges was the regular first baseman on the 1949, '52, '53, '55, '56, and '59 National League champions. From 1949 through 1955 Hodges drove in over 100 runs seven straight seasons. He was a lifetime .273 hitter.

SECOND BASE ★ JACKIE ROBINSON

Jack Roosevelt Robinson is not only one of the most sociologically important players in baseball history, he was also an outstanding performer. As the first black in modern baseball, Robinson blazed a trail for all Ameri- cans. As a Brooklyn Dodger, he was the 1947 Rookie of the Year, the 1949 National League MVP and batting champion, and a lifetime .311 hitter for his 10 seasons in Brooklyn. He was a tough clutch hitter and an unsettling base runner who twice led the NL in stolen bases.

SHORTSTOP ★ PEE WEE REESE

For 16 seasons, Harold (Pee Wee) Reese was the premier shortstop in the National League. He was not only an outstanding defensive player but also an aggressive base runner and a timely hitter who had 885 career RBIs. Reese generally had 20 or more stolen bases in an era when that was a high total and led the league with 30 in 1952. In 1949 he had a league-high 132 runs scored, and in 1954 he had his best year as a hitter, batting .309.

THIRD BASE ★ RON CEY

During most of the period from 1971 to 1982, Ron Cey was the regular third baseman for the Dodgers, and during most of that time he ranked among the National League's best run-producers. He is the all-time leader for the club with 1,468 games at third base, and he hit 228 home runs for the Dodgers, more than any other Dodger since the team's move to Los Angeles in 1958. He collected 842 runs batted in and 2,321 total bases. Cey was a six-time choice for the NL All-Star team and shared the 1981 World Series MVP Award.

LEFT FIELD ★ ZACH WHEAT

For 18 seasons Zach Wheat was the Dodgers' regular left fielder, and during that time the team won two National League pennants (1916 and 1920). Wheat won a batting championship (1918) when he hit .335. A lifetime .317 hitter, Wheat batted over .300 13 times in 18 seasons, including totals of .375 and .359 in 1924 and 1925. He began his career in 1909 and hit .304 as a rookie, going on to collect 2,884 career hits, including 476 doubles and 172 triples (both are still Dodger club records). He also remains the only player in Dodger history to amass over 4,000 total bases in his career.

CENTER FIELD ★ DUKE SNIDER

Edwin Donald Snider was the lone left-handed bat in a Brooklyn lineup loaded with right-handed power. But he more than made up for this imbalance by hitting 407 career home runs, driving in 1,333 runs, and hitting .295 for his 18-year tour in the National League. In the 1950s Snider was one of the top power hitters in the league, hitting 40 or more home runs five straight seasons from 1953 to 1957. He led the league with 43 in 1956 and might have hit appreciably more in his career except that the configuration of the L.A. Coliseum (where the Dodgers played for four years after moving from Brooklyn) worked against him.

RIGHT FIELD ★ CARL FURILLO

Perhaps the most underrated of the post–World War II Dodger outfielders, Furillo was a superb outfielder with a celebrated arm, which brought him one of his nicknames, the Reading Rifle (he was from Reading, Pa.). His other nickname, "Skoonj," referred to his Italian heritage. Furillo joined the Dodgers in 1946 and played 15 seasons with the club. He was the National League batting champion in 1953 (.344) and hit .299 lifetime for the Dodgers with 1,910 hits, including 192 homers, 1,058 RBIs, and 2,922 total bases.

CATCHER ★ ROY CAMPANELLA

For 10 years, before his career was tragically cut short by an automobile accident, Roy Campanella ranked as one of the best catchers in baseball. During his three greatest years, he was the league MVP. In 1951 he hit .325 with 33 homers and 108 RBIs. In 1953 he hit .312, led the league with 142 RBIs, and had a career-high 41 homers. In 1955 he hit .318 with 32 homers and 107 RBIs. Overall, Campy had 242 homers in 10 seasons and batted .276 for his career. He played on five pennant-winning clubs, including the 1955 World Champions.

LEFT-HANDED STARTER ★ SANDY KOUFAX

During his prime years, Brooklyn-born Sandy Koufax was the finest left-hander in the major leagues. In his final four years, Koufax won 97 games and lost only 27, a .782 winning percentage. He led the league in ERA five straight seasons before arm and elbow problems ended his career. In 1963 he was 25-5; in 1965 he was 26-8; and in 1966 he was 27-9. During his last four seasons, he struck out 1,228 men in 1,193 innings. He helped pitch the Dodgers to pennants in 1959, '63, '65, and '66. He pitched four no-hitters (including a perfect game), won three Cy Young Awards, and was the 1963 NL MVP.

RIGHT-HANDED STARTER ★ DON DRYSDALE

A towering presence on the mound and an intimidating demeanor helped Don Drysdale to a 209-166 career and a 2.95 career ERA that included the longest shutout streak in major league history, 58⅔ innings in 1968. His finest season, however, was 1962, when he was 25-9 and led the league in strikeouts for the third time in four years with 232. Paired with Koufax, Drysdale helped the Dodgers win four pennants: 1959, '63, '65, and '66. The team just missed in 1962, losing a playoff series to the Giants after tying for the league lead.

RELIEF PITCHER ★ JIM BREWER

From 1964 to 1975 Jim Brewer was a part of one of the best pitching staffs in the majors. He came to play a leading role on that staff as the late-inning relief specialist now known as the closer. Brewer appeared in 474 games for the Dodgers and recorded 125 saves, the most in the history of the club. He led the Dodgers in saves six straight seasons from 1968 through 1973, with 20 or more saves in four of those six seasons.

RECORD HOLDERS

CAREER

BATTING

Games	Zack Wheat	2,322
At-bats	Zack Wheat	8,859
Batting average	Willie Keeler	.360
Runs	Pee Wee Reese	1,338
Hits	Zack Wheat	2,804
Doubles	Zack Wheat	464
Triples	Zack Wheat	171
Home runs	Duke Snider	389
Grand slams	Gil Hodges	12
Total bases	Zack Wheat	4,003
Slugging percentage	Duke Snider	.553
RBIs	Duke Snider	1,271
Extra-base hits	Duke Snider	814
Bases on balls	Ron Cey	765
Strikeouts	Duke Snider	1,123
Stolen bases	Maury Wills	490

PITCHING

Games	Don Sutton	550
Wins	Don Sutton	233
Losses	Don Sutton	181
Starts	Don Sutton	533
Complete games	Brickyard Kennedy	279
Shutouts	Don Sutton	52
Innings	Don Sutton	3,814
ERA	Jeff Pfeffer	2.31
Strikeouts	Don Sutton	2,696
Walks	Brickyard Kennedy	1,128
Saves	Jim Brewer	125
Relief appearances	Jim Brewer	491
Winning percentage	Sandy Koufax	.655

Zack Wheat

Photo: National Baseball Library, Cooperstown, N.Y.

Don Sutton

RECORD HOLDERS

SEASON

BATTING

Games	Maury Wills (1962)	165
At-bats	Maury Wills (1962)	695
Batting average	Babe Herman (1930)	.393
Runs	Hub Collins (1890)	148
Hits	Babe Herman (1930)	241
Doubles	Johnny Frederick (1929)	52
Triples	George Treadway (1894)	26
Home runs	Duke Snider (1956)	43
Grand slams*	Mike Sciosia (1989)	2
Total bases	Babe Herman (1930)	416
Slugging percentage	Babe Herman (1930)	.678
RBIs	Tommy Davis (1962)	153
Extra-base hits	Babe Herman (1930)	94
Bases on balls	Eddie Stankey (1945)	148
Most strikeouts	Billy Grabarkewitz (1970)	149
Fewest Strikeouts	Jim Johnson (1923)	15
Stolen bases	Maury Wills (1962)	104

*This record has been previously achieved by 15 other Dodgers.

PITCHING

Games	Mike Marshall (1974)	106
Wins	Tom Lovett (1890)	30
Losses	George Bell (1910)	27
Starts	William Terry (1890), George Haddock (1892), Brickyard Kennedy (1893)	44
Complete games	Brickyard Kennedy (1893)	40
Shutouts	Sandy Koufax (1963)	11
Innings	Brickyard Kennedy (1893)	382⅔
ERA	Rube Marquard (1916)	1.58
Strikeouts	Sandy Koufax (1965)	382
Walks	Bill Donovan (1901)	151
Saves	Jay Howell (1989)	28
Relief appearances	Mike Marshall (1974)	106
Winning percentage	Preacher Row (1951)	.880

TRIVIA QUIZ

1. In 1974 this Dodger became the first relief pitcher to win the Cy Young Award. Name him.

2. From 1979 to 1982 the Dodgers won the Rookie of the Year Award all four years. Name the four players.

3. This famous Dodger catcher won the National League Most Valuable Player awards in three odd-numbered years. Who was he?

4. Besides New York and California, what state have the Dodgers played regular-season home games in?

5. This Dodger pitcher had eight shutouts to lead the National League in 1989. Name him.

6. On June 4, 1972, the Dodgers retired three uniform numbers in the same ceremony. Who were the players whose numbers were retired?

7. This man managed the Dodgers on 23 one-year contracts. Who was he?

8. In 1930 this Dodger outfielder batted .393 but did not win the batting title. Who was he?

9. Which one-time Dodger manager also managed the New York Yankees and the New York Mets?

10. Only one Dodger has topped 2,000 career hits while the team was based in Los Angeles. Name him.

ANSWERS ON PAGE 63

1991 SCHEDULE

APRIL

SUN	MON	TUE	WED	THU	FRI	SAT
	1	2	3	4	5 **CAL** 7:35	6 **CAL** 7:05
7 **CAL** 1:05	8	9 **ATL** 4:40	10 **ATL** 4:40	11 **ATL** 11:10	12 **SD** 1:05	13 **SD** 7:05
14 **SD** 1:05	15 **SF** 7:05	16 **SF** 7:35	17 **SF** 12:35	18 **SD** 1:05	19 **SD** 7:05	20 **SD** 7:05
21 **SD** 1:05	22 **ATL** 7:35	23 **ATL** 7:35	24 **ATL** 7:35	25 **SF** 7:35	26 **SF** 7:35	27 **SF** 7:05
28 **SF** 1:05	29	30 **MON** 4:35				

MAY

SUN	MON	TUE	WED	THU	FRI	SAT
			1 **MON** 4:35	2	3 **PHI** 4:35	4 **PHI** 4:05
5 **PHI** 10:35	6	7 **NY** 4:40	8 **NY** 4:40	9	10 **PHI** 7:35	11 **PHI** 7:05
12 **PHI** 1:05	13 **MON** 7:35	14 **MON** 7:35	15 **MON** 7:35	16	17 **NY** 7:35	18 **NY** 12:15
19 **NY** 1:05	20 **HOU** 5:35	21 **HOU** 5:35	22 **HOU** 5:35	23 **HOU** 4:05	24 **CIN** 4:35	25 **CIN** 10:15
26 **CIN** 11:15	27 **HOU** 7:35	28 **HOU** 7:35	29 **HOU** 7:35	30 **CIN** 7:35	31 **CIN** 7:35	

JUNE

SUN	MON	TUE	WED	THU	FRI	SAT
						1 **CIN** 7:05
2 **CIN** 1:05	3	4 **STL** 5:35	5 **STL** 5:35	6 **STL** 5:35	7 **CHI** 12:20	8 **CHI** 11:20
9 **CHI** 11:20	10 **CHI** 5:05	11 **PIT** 4:35	12 **PIT** 4:35	13 **PIT** 12:05	14 **STL** 7:35	15 **STL** 7:05
16 **STL** 1:05	17 **CHI** 7:35	18 **CHI** 7:35	19 **CHI** 7:35	20 **PIT** 7:35	21 **PIT** 7:35	22 **PIT** 12:15
23 **PIT** 1:05	24	25 **SF** 7:35	26 **SF** 7:35	27	28 **ATL** 4:40	29 **ATL** 4:10
30 **ATL** 5:05						

☐ Home games   ☐ Road games

JULY

SUN	MON	TUE	WED	THU	FRI	SAT
	1	2 **SD** 7:05	3 **SD** 7:05	4 **SD** 7:05	5 **ATL** 7:35	6 **ATL** 7:05
7 **ATL** 1:05	8	9 ALL-STAR GAME	10	11 **MON** 4:35	12 **MON** 4:35	13 **MON** 4:35
14 **MON** 10:35	15 **PHI** 4:35	16 **PHI** 4:35	17 **PHI** 9:35	18 **NY** 4:40	19 **NY** 4:40	20 **NY** 10:15
21 **NY** 10:40	22	23 **PHI** 7:35	24 **PHI** 7:35	25 **PHI** 7:35	26 **MON** 7:35	27 **MON** 7:05
28 **MON** 1:05	29 **NY** 7:35	30 **NY** 7:35	31 **NY** 7:35			

AUGUST

SUN	MON	TUE	WED	THU	FRI	SAT
				1	2 **HOU** 5:35	3 **HOU** 5:05
4 **HOU** 11:35	5 **CIN** 4:35	6 **CIN** 4:35	7 **CIN** 4:35	8 **CIN** 9:35	9 **SF** 7:35	10 **SF** 1:05
11 **SF** 1:05	12 **CIN** 7:35	13 **CIN** 7:35	14 **CIN** 7:35	15 **HOU** 7:35	16 **HOU** 7:35	17 **HOU** 7:05
18 **HOU** 1:05	19 **SD** 7:35	20 **SD** 7:35	21 **SD** 1:05	22	23 **STL** 5:35	24 **STL** 5:05
25 **STL** 11:15	26 **CHI** 5:05	27 **CHI** 11:20	28 **PIT** 7:35	29 **PIT** 7:35	30 **CHI** 7:35	31 **CHI** 7:05

SEPTEMBER

SUN	MON	TUE	WED	THU	FRI	SAT
1 **CHI** 1:05	2 **STL** 7:35	3 **STL** 7:35	4 **STL** 7:35	5	6 **PIT** 4:35	7 **PIT** 4:05
8 **PIT** 10:35	9 **CIN** 4:35	10 **CIN** 4:35	11 **HOU** 5:35	12 **HOU** 4:05	13 **ATL** 4:40	14 **ATL** 4:10
15 **ATL** 11:10	16 **CIN** 7:35	17 **CIN** 7:35	18 **HOU** 7:35	19 **HOU** 1:05	20 **ATL** 7:35	21 **ATL** 7:05
22 **ATL** 1:05	23	24 **SD** 7:05	25 **SD** 7:05	26	27 **SF** 7:35	28 **SF** 12:15
29 **SF** 5:05	30 **SD** 7:35					

OCTOBER

SUN	MON	TUE	WED	THU	FRI	SAT
		1 **SD** 7:35	2 **SD** 7:35	3	4 **SF** 7:35	5 **SF** 1:05
6 **SF** 1:05	7	8	9	10	11	12

Times Listed are PST

COLLECTOR'S CORNER

NOTES
&
AUTOGRAPHS

Ain't no fences high enough.

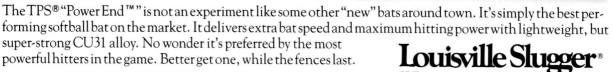

The TPS® "Power End™" is not an experiment like some other "new" bats around town. It's simply the best performing softball bat on the market. It delivers extra bat speed and maximum hitting power with lightweight, but super-strong CU31 alloy. No wonder it's preferred by the most powerful hitters in the game. Better get one, while the fences last.

Louisville Slugger®

H&B Hillerich & Bradsby Co. Louisville, Kentucky